100%
UNOFFICIAL

First published in Great Britain 2024 by
100% Unofficial, a part of Farshore

An imprint of HarperCollins*Publishers*
1 London Bridge Street, London SE1 9GF
www.farshore.co.uk

HarperCollins*Publishers*
Macken House,
39/40 Mayor Street Upper,
Dublin 1 D01 C9W8, Ireland

Written by Craig Jelley
Illustrated by Matt Burgess

This book is an original creation by Farshore
© 2024 HarperCollinsPublishers Limited

All rights in the FORTNITE game, including rights in the images taken from the
FORTNITE game, are owned by Epic Games Inc.. This book is an unofficial guide to the
FORTNITE game. This book is published by Farshore; neither this book nor Farshore
is associated with or affiliated with Epic Games Inc.
All in-game images © 2024 Epic Games Inc.

ISBN 978 0 00 864661 5
Printed and bound in Romania
001

ONLINE SAFETY FOR YOUNGER FANS

Spending time online is great fun! Here are a few simple rules to help younger fans stay safe and
keep the internet a great place to spend time:

- Never give out your real name – don't use it as your username.
- Never give out any of your personal details.
- Never tell anybody which school you go to or how old you are.
- Never tell anybody your password except a parent or a guardian.
- Be aware that you must be 13 or over to create an account on many sites.
Always check the site policy and ask a parent or guardian for permission before registering.
- Always tell a parent or guardian if something is worrying you.

Stay safe online. Any website addresses listed in this book are correct at the time of going to print.
However, Farshore is not responsible for content hosted by third parties. Please be aware that online
content can be subject to change and websites can contain content that is unsuitable for children.
We advise that all children are supervised when using the internet.

Stay safe online. Farshore is not responsible for content hosted by third parties.

This book contains FSC™ certified paper and other controlled
sources to ensure responsible forest management.

For more information visit: www.harpercollins.co.uk/green

100% UNOFFICIAL

FORTNITE
ANNUAL 2025

CONTENTS

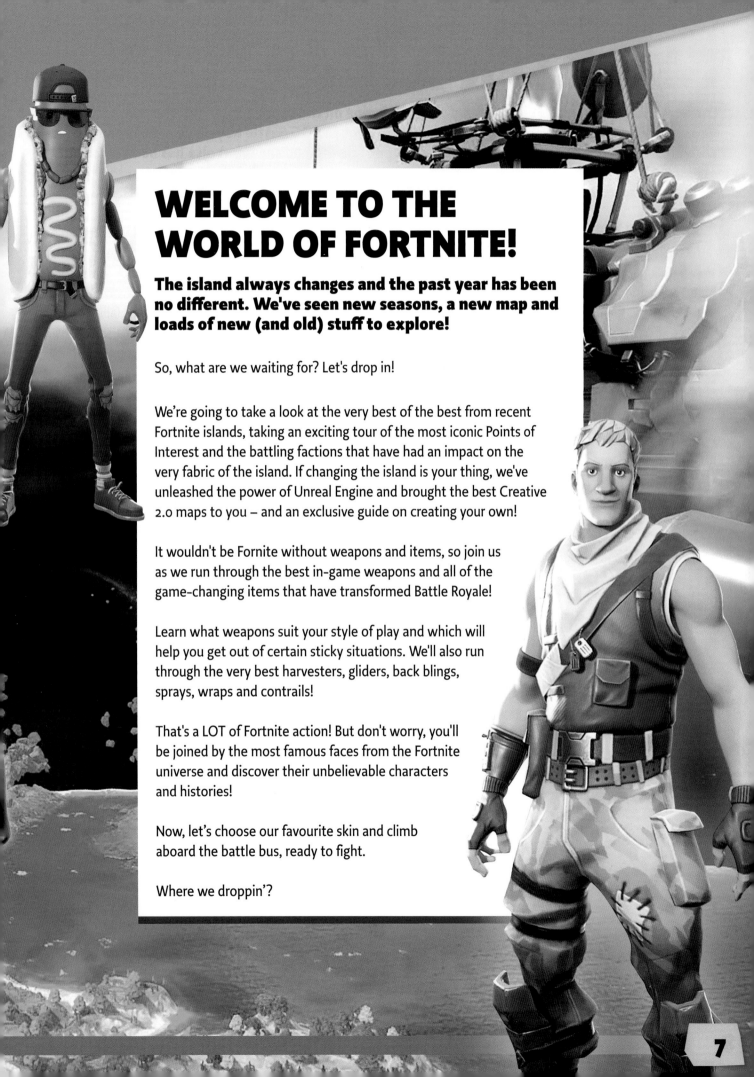

WELCOME TO THE WORLD OF FORTNITE!

The island always changes and the past year has been no different. We've seen new seasons, a new map and loads of new (and old) stuff to explore!

So, what are we waiting for? Let's drop in!

We're going to take a look at the very best of the best from recent Fortnite islands, taking an exciting tour of the most iconic Points of Interest and the battling factions that have had an impact on the very fabric of the island. If changing the island is your thing, we've unleashed the power of Unreal Engine and brought the best Creative 2.0 maps to you – and an exclusive guide on creating your own!

It wouldn't be Fornite without weapons and items, so join us as we run through the best in-game weapons and all of the game-changing items that have transformed Battle Royale!

Learn what weapons suit your style of play and which will help you get out of certain sticky situations. We'll also run through the very best harvesters, gliders, back blings, sprays, wraps and contrails!

That's a LOT of Fortnite action! But don't worry, you'll be joined by the most famous faces from the Fortnite universe and discover their unbelievable characters and histories!

Now, let's choose our favourite skin and climb aboard the battle bus, ready to fight.

Where we droppin'?

CHAPTER RECAP

The last year of Fortnite has been a wild ride, beginning on the completely new island of Asteria and then coming to an end … back where we started. Yes, we got the OG Battle Royale island back and it was a hit with players old and new. Let's take a look at recent seasons and see what else has been going on!

SEASON 1

After plotting for the majority of Chapter 3, The Herald was able to begin breaking up the island and dismantling it. Luckily for us, the Loopers managed to piece back together the island from a Zero Point, but it sucked in pieces from other realities. Returning players landed on Asteria, the medieval-themed version of the island ruled by the Oathbound, an ancient precursor of the evil Imagined Order … what a start!

The map was covered in olde-worlde locations like Anvil Square and Brutal Bastion. Players could get their hands on new pseudo-primitive weaponry, such as the sword-shooting Ex-Caliber Rifle and the Shockwave Hammer, which sends players flying and buildings falling apart, but allows you to bounce! Players could also now use Reality Augments, which gives them a buff – such as faster reloads and bonus damage – every few minutes during a match.

GAME-CHANGERS

Primal Flame Bow

Ex-Caliber Rifle

Shockwave Hammer

GAME-CHANGERS

Nitro Drifter

Kinetic Blade

Overclocked Pulse Rifle

SEASON 2

The island received a glow-up in Season 2, with the neon-tinted metropolis of MEGA City appearing from the red rift that cracked the sky in Season 1, along with loads of Japanese-themed locations. The crack closed up over the now-futuristic island as Evie attempted to band the factions together to stop The Last Reality in their quest to return the Omniverse to nothing. The island and the action were an incredible combinaton.

As well as the new neon glow covering the island, players found a couple of new ways to get around. The first were the grind rails that criss-crossed MEGA City, which players could move along effortlessly, taking shots while they travelled along the rail. But the best new movement methods were on wheels – two new vehicles were added: Nitro Drifter and Victory Crown Rogue. The first is a car that you can drift on, while the latter is a motorbike that lets you do a sweet low slide!

CHAPTER RECAP

GAME-CHANGERS

Kinetic Boomerang

Enhanced Flapjack Rifle

Cybertron Cannon

SEASON 3

The island had already begun to crack due to events in the previous season and in Season 3, the centre of the island collapsed, revealing a long-forgotten jungle below. Nature took over Asteria, with vines and flora sprawling across the map, but they weren't the only new arrivals. A group called The Explorers were already investigating the jungle and the ruins dotted within them. They agreed to help decipher the nature of The Apparatus, an ancient projector that could hold the key to the rifts.

Several ruins emerged from the map and with them came a whole host of research stations, presumably set up by The Explorers. Grind rails that had appeared beyond MEGA City disappeared in place of grind vines and weapons became a little more basic too; Kinetic Boomerangs flew back and forth across the jungle in battle. Although there was still the addition of the explosive Cybertron Cannon which dealt quick-fire splash damage in a constant barrage!

SEASON 4

As if battling against evil factions among the threat of time rifts wasn't enough, Season 4 dropped Kado Thorne, a time-travelling vampire, into the mix after the sun was blotted out during the Eclipse event. The recently reformed Slone enlists the help of Nolan Chance to help steal Thorne's time machine and a season full of heist shenanigans was in full swing. Once they get their hands on the machine, they realise Thorne has set it to go back in time five years.

The map got a little bit darker with Thorne's arrival – the moody locations of Sanguine Suites, Eclipsed Estate and Frenzy fields appeared at the same time as the moody vamp. You could pick up keycards for vaults dotted all around the island and deploy some clever espionage weaponry during your infiltration, if you wanted to be sneaky. The Business Turret appears to be just a simple metallic briefcase, however, when thrown it will transform into your own personal turret.

GAME-CHANGERS

Rocket Ram

Business Turret

Nitro Fang

GAME-CHANGERS

Damage Trap

Port-A-Fort

SEASON 5

Once the Time Machine was in the hands of Slone, they managed to bring back items and objects to the map that had been part of the original island. After Kado's tinkering with the machine it set a course for the past and the time machine warped reality back to Chapter 1 ... sort of. It appears that some things aren't exactly as they should be. Could it be that the heroes have found their way into an alternate past?

Fan-favourite locations like Tilted Towers, Retail Row and Loot Lake reclaimed their places on the OG map, but they weren't the only things to return. The Damage Trap dropped back into the rotation of items, along with basic vehicles like the Shopping Cart and the All Terrain Kart. Weapons were returned back to basics too – LMGs, Burst Assault Rifles, Heavy Shotguns and more could be found in chests and floor loot. So much fun!

WHERE WE DROPPIN'?

With all the interesting inventions that Epic has made to the Battle Royale island, whether it's travelling back in time or destroying it completely, they really outdid themselves in Season 5 when they returned the map to its original state. Let's take a look back at what the OG Island had to offer.

RETAIL ROW

If it's loot you're after then firstly, you're playing the game correctly, but secondly, the shops of Retail Row are incredibly well-stocked, so consider dropping here and ransacking the Row.

SEASON FIVE

The OG map from Chapter 4 Season 5 wasn't the very first Battle Royale map, it was actually an exact replica of Chapter 1 Season 5. You can tell by the inclusion of places like Dusty Divot, which weren't around at the beginning.

PLEASANT PARK

The spacious suburban quarter of the Island has lots of impressive houses surrounding the open greenery, meaning it's perfect for luring enemies out into the open.

LOOT LAKE

For those that prefer to see their opponents coming, the shores of Loot Lake offered the opportunity to see enemies dropping for miles around, before crafting their master plan.

DUSTY DIVOT

This scientific research station sprang up in the middle of a crater caused by a massive impact. Unfortunately, it's still home to the odd explosion from launchers and remote explosives.

HOT SPOTS

Battle Royalers who had seen the map already will have known exactly where to drop for different purposes, but for everyone else, these locations were just as alien as brand new locations. Let's level the playing field and look closer at the OG locations.

CLASSY COURTS

Positioned on the north of the island amongst snow-covered trees and arctic conditions, Classy Courts is the perfect place to unwind and practise your tennis serve. How that will help you achieve a Victory Royale, we don't know ... but it sure is pretty! Watch out for enemies creeping between the courts, and don't get scared when you enter the location's creepy teddy bear factory!

RUINED REELS

No one knows the origins of this ancient ampitheatre, sandwiched between Fencing Fields and Lavish Lair. Whilst its theatrical performances may have finished many years ago, it was always putting on a show on the Fortnite island. Players would gather in front of its stadium seating and perform epic takedowns in front of the huge cinema screen!

FENCING FIELDS

This area of farmland might look unassuming, but it is actually a key provider of one of the island's favourite consumables. It is the sole producer of Flowberries, which add 15 shield points and the effect of anti-gravity for a few seconds. Hidden amongst the stylish farm buildings were a whopping 82 loot chests – making this a great place to drop in!

LAVISH LAIR

This impressive mansion and surrounding grounds is a sight to behold, and will tempt any curious battler in to explore. But be warned, it was heavily guarded by Oscar and The Society. With sparse loot and maze-like corridors, it was best viewed from afar. Unless you're planning on staying for the long haul? Just remember to turn the heating on.

RITZY RIVIERA

This glamorous seaside location was a big hit with those who valued the finer things in life. No, we aren't talking about the yachts lining the marina walls or the fancy villas - we're talking about the abundance of loot hidden there - especially in the Vault! Having said that, after a hard few minutes looting, it would be nice to cool off under the shade of a palm tree on the beach. Ah, bliss!

CLOISTERED CASTLE

From its strategic position next to the sea, Cloistered Castle suited gamers that play with a defensive style. It seemed this mysterious island castle was good at keeping secrets hidden, too – many players believe Kado Thorne owned it. The evidence is the enormous stash of Chapter 4 props inside and the huge portrait of Kado hanging in one of the rooms. That's a good clue, we guess!

REBEL'S ROOST

This sprawling mansion was once an impressive residence but has since been abandoned and fallen into a state of disrepair. In recent times, the rebel group known as The Underground have taken it over as one of their many hidden hideouts across the island. We wonder if they'll ever clean off all the graffiti that can be seen lining the corridors or even tend to the garden.

HOT SPOTS

THE MARIGOLD

It should come as no surprise that this majestic yacht is now owned by The Society, who are as corrupt as they are wealthy! Although it's a good base for defensive-minded players, you'll notice that opponents are able to rush over to its deck on the two ziplines, so you'd be well advised to keep an eye on the horizon, captain!

SHIP IT! STATION

If you are a fan of importing and exporting goods, then ... why are you playing Fortnite so much? This warehouse building is made up of three floors and is the head office of the company Ship It! Although the workforce have vanished, it looks just as operational as always. Explore the server room for high-tech loot or simply use this large structure as a big place to hide from any nearby enemies.

UNDERGROUND HQ

This abandoned underground train station is one of the bases belonging to The Underground, and is their chief headquarters. Their aim is to take down all of the leaders of The Society and you'll find a Bounty Board stashed here, showing all the leaders they're currently hunting. The atmosphere down there might be cold but it sure is cool!

RESEARCH ROCK

Hidden away on the southeastern edge of the island, this was the primary base for the The Explorers. This group of researchers left it pretty well stocked, too. There are living quarters, research rooms and even a warehouse full of supplies – making it a desirable landing location, despite its perilous position on the edge of the map.

SUMMIT BASE CAMP

Situated just down from Superior Summit – the tallest mountain on the island – Summit Base Camp was only for the bravest players, with barely any defensive structures or resources. What it lacked in chests and looting opportunities, it made up for with unbeatable views of the surrounding island.

SANDY STRIP

No one is quite sure why you would build an airport runway on a beach, but that doesn't stop loads of players coming in to land at Sandy Strip. This landmark was always fun to explore, but its position on the edge of the map made it more difficult to escape the shrinking storm circle. You could always fly into the safe zone though, couldn't you?

THE TRAIN

One of the most unique locations on the island, The Train actually travels along its tracks! Whilst it moves at a faster speed than you can run, it slows down when it approaches stations, so use that opportunity to jump aboard. A full loop of the island takes nine minutes, so make sure you're safe from the storm and keep an eye out for other enemies onboard!

PLAY YOUR WAY

You can't just 'play Fortnite' now, because the game has evolved to be so big and to incorporate so many different ways of playing. It could mean chilling out and making a cool map or battling hordes of AI-controlled enemies with your friends. Here are a few of the best ways to 'play Fortnite'.

BATTLE ROYALE

You know the drill by now, because this is the mode that launched Fortnite into the gaming stratosphere! One hundred of the finest warriors drop onto the island, scavenge for supplies and weapons and shoot their way to the final rounds, avoiding the storm circle in the process.

RANKED PLAY

If you want to see how you compare to other players, you can play ranked versions of Battle Royale and Zero Build. As you eliminate enemies and place highly in matches, you'll climb from the lowly depths of Bronze to the highest tier, Unreal. Only if you're good enough though ...

ZERO BUILD

For the more traditional fan of shooting games, Epic introduced the Zero Build mode in Chapter 3, Season 2. It took away the building element, so that the centurions on the island had only their shooting skills to rely on. It was only meant to be in the game temporarily, but it was so popular, Epic left it in as a playable game mode.

GO IT ALONE?

As well as the different game modes, you can change the way you play the game simply by whether you're going solo or battling with a few trusted friends by your side.

SOLO

It's every player for themselves if you're dropping onto the island on your own. If you're playing Solo, it's you versus the world, so you need to be a jack of all trades – building, shooting, scavenging, running away from the storm circle, screaming and so on. Nobody has your back here – you will need to think tactically to pass the test of survival!

DUO

Grab your best pal and explore the island in tandem to make things a little less lonely and give yourself a better chance of survival. Your partner can revive you, share the spoils of their scavenging so you're both wielding the best equipment and help you eliminate enemies on the battlefield.

SQUADS

The most chaotic way to play is to grab three buddies and blaze a trail through the map. Sure, you could build epic sniper towers and execute an amazing strategy, but you could also grab some Legendary weapons, hop in a vehicle and annihilate the opposition on the way to Victory Royale.

SAVE THE WORLD

Though it's available separately to the core Battle Royale version of Fortnite, Save the World shares a lot of the same mechanics as Battle Royale. It has the same weapons, building and teamwork for up to four players, but you're not fighting against enemy teams: this time you're fighting waves of randomly generated monsters. Can you survive?

PLAY YOUR WAY

Now you've seen the classic ways to play Fortnite, let's mix it up a bit with these additional modes. The objectives might be different, and you might not even set foot on the island, but they're all excellent fun – just like Battle Royale.

ROCKET RACING

Games don't come much faster than this supersonic arcade racing game! You can drift, fly and boost your way around epic circuits and put your skills to the ultimate test of speed. In Speed Run mode, you simply have to set the fastest lap time around tracks set amongst the island's most iconic locations. Do your best and check your times against players around the world!

DESERTED: DOMINATION

Epic's answer to the iconic Capture the Flag is Deserted: Domination. It pits two teams of five against each other on an Unreal-made map as they try to wrestle control of tactical points away from the opposing team over six rounds. You need to pick one of seven different classes, each with a unique loadout, to help your team complete the objective.

TEAM RUMBLE

Isn't it annoying when you collect an inventory full of legendary gear and someone sneaks up with a shotgun and ends you? Well fortunately, Team Rumble has infinite respawns! You play as part of a 16-person team and simply compete to get the most eliminations over a certain period of time. The team with the most eliminations wins!

CREATIVE

Breathe a sigh of relief because, for once, there aren't any enemies trying to end you! In Creative mode, you've got every building, weapon, trap and doodad at your fingertips – you can use these to create interesting maps to 1v1 your friends, or add rules and boundaries to make your own minigame to release into the wild.

CREATIVE 2.0

In Season X, Epic released Creative 2.0, which incorporates the power of Unreal Engine, so developers and modders can make even more impressive minigames. If you want to take your minigame to the next level, download the Unreal Editor for Fortnite.

PARTY ROYALE

If there's an event on the horizon, chances are it'll take place in the Party Royale game mode, which has hosted concerts from DJs like Steve Aoki and Deadmau5 in the past. When there isn't an awesome DJ spinning the wheels of steel, you can drop by Party Royale for a spot of fishing, play a game of football or take part in a boat race. Why would you ever need to leave?

GOLDEN RULES

You, me and millions of others have been dropping on to Fortnite's island for over seven years now! Even though it has changed dramatically, there are some things that remain the same when you're fighting for the holy grail: Victory Royale!

CHOOSE YOUR DROP

After a few drops – and our helpful location guide on page 14 – you'll have sussed out all the different areas of the island and what each one is good for. Don't wait for the Battle Bus to kick you out: pick a location, jump as soon as you can and beat the other players down to your favourite drop spot – so you can get all the swag before them.

LOOT THEN SHOOT

If you land in a popular location, it's likely that you'll be surrounded by dozens of enemies too. You might be tempted to engage them straight away, but focus on getting materials and loot first. Your enemy might have lucked out and got their hands on a legendary shotgun at the start, which will easily beat you and the common revolver you found on the ground ...

INVENTORY MANAGEMENT

Once you start looting, you need to be careful about which items you're carrying with you. There's no point having an inventory full of weapons – even in the unlikely event that they're all legendary. Share the best weapons with your duo or squad and make sure that you're carrying a couple of healing items and another non-gun offensive item like dynamite – anything that could give you the element of surprise if things aren't going your way.

AVOID THE STORM

When the storm forms around you, keep a constant eye on where it is, and more importantly, where it's going to be. It's a very smart move to hunker down in safety and wait to pick off enemies passing by, but it's the opposite if your base is about to be passed by the approaching storm wall! Keep your operation on the move and choose buildings as temporary bases as you travel.

BUILD TO WIN

It's very easy to pick up a gun and eliminate the enemy, but if that enemy starts building walls, ramps and towers before your eyes, the job becomes a lot harder. The end stages of a Battle Royale often come down to who has the better building skills, so practise throwing up walls and ramps throughout the round and editing them on the fly to give yourself the advantage in the dying stages of the storm.

BACK TO BASICS: BUILDS

If you want to rank among the very best Fortnite players, you'll need to master building. Pros can throw up incredibly complicated structures in just a few minutes and construct defences on the fly between firing off rounds of bullets at the enemy. Let's take it back to basics and look at what you can do with some simple materials.

COLLECTING MATERIALS

Before you can build your first wall, you're going to need something to build with. There are three materials in Fortnite - wood, stone and metal – and you can destroy pretty much everything on the island with your harvesting tool to get your hands on these. Stronger materials take longer to break, so make sure you're aiming for the sweet red spot in the reticule when you're swinging your tool.

STRENGTH OR SPEED

You can build any structure from any of the three materials, but the one you choose will have different stats. Wood is the easiest to harvest and takes the least time to build, but it has the lowest strength. If you favour a strong build over speed, then metal will take much more damage before it's destroyed, while stone occupies a happy middle ground between the two.

EDITING BUILDINGS

As you're surviving your way through each match, you might spot an existing building and think something like, 'that would be a perfect base, if only it had a window'. Well luckily for you and your bright ideas, you can edit any building you see! Just press the edit button and cycle through the different types of wall, floors, roofs and stairs to change the building you're looking at.

BASIC BUILD SHAPES

You can't build anything without knowing what tools you have to work with, so let's take a quick look at the basic features that you can construct during a Battle Royale.

WALLS

The basic upright building block that you'll probably use more often than any other. As well as being great for building solid bases, it's a superb shield to throw up if you're being pelted with bullets. You can also edit in windows and doors to peek through, too.

FLOORS

If you plan to make a tall building like a sniper's post, the chances are that you'll need to throw down a floor or two. They can be edited to remove any of the quarters, so you can basically add trapdoors for a quick getaway if you need to escape.

STAIRS

Sometimes called ramps, the stairs are a very useful feature to add to tall buildings, though they're also useful for traversing cliffs, whether you're travelling up or down. They can be edited to add turns, which makes it easier to drop and hide if attacked.

ROOFS

These building-toppers are great for protecting you against hails of bullets from above, particularly if you're building in the lowlands of the island. The basic pyramid shape is also good for creating a half-wall that provides protection and a shooting opportunity.

ZERO BUILD

If you just can't get the hang of building, you can try the Zero Build Battle Royale, which has been around since Chapter 3, Season 2 and bans the building side of the game!

USEFUL STRUCTURES

Now we've had a refresher on the basic building blocks of Fortnite, let's take a look at a few structures you can put together to help you defend yourself or give you an advantage in attack!

THE BOX

Your builds don't have to be pretty, as long as they serve a purpose. The basic box, which is just four walls and a roof, can be the difference between life and death if you're low on health and need just a few seconds to chug a shield potion or apply some bandages. Practise quickly spinning around and throwing up those walls and you'll be a box master in no time.

PEEKABOO BOX

This structure is perfect for setting up on an elevated position. You can walk up the internal ramp to scout an area and take shots at enemies, then back down again to hide when they start shooting back. The door at the bottom of the ramp means you have a quick exit if anyone invades or manages to get a higher vantage point than you.

LOOKOUT TOWER

If you don't have the high ground in a firefight, you can make it instead. Build this structure as tall as you need to so you can level the battlefield when being attacked from cliffs or skyscrapers. Each level should have half-turn stairs to make it easy to ascend and descend – not to mention break your fall if the top windowed layer is destroyed during the battle.

SHOOTING GALLERY

Perfect for solos, but especially effective for a squad of four, this build utilises pyramid roofs as floors to give players a way to easily pop up and shoot anyone heading in their direction. It's especially confusing if the enemy sees people popping up in four different places, and it's great to build it across a narrow passage, especially when the storm is forcing people down your particular bottleneck ...

SHIELDED RAMP

Building stairs is a great way to get the high ground advantage on the enemy, but it can be easy to pick you off if others are up high too. As you build stairs, add walls to the side so you can still reach the high ground but with some defence, too. It's wise to build the ramp in pairs too so that it's harder for enemies to completely destroy your structure and bring you tumbling down.

CREATIVE MODE MAPS 1

In March of 2023, Epic Games released Creative 2.0, which incorporated Unreal Engine into the Creative experience. This allowed super-smart minigame-makers to create even smarter minigames for the Fortnite community to enjoy. Let's take a look at a few of the best.

ROCKET WARS 2 (5196-0233-5799)

Join one of four teams on your very own private rocket launch platform. Here, you'll work together to protect your spacefaring vehicle, whilst trying to sabotage the enemy teams' vessels. Use the launchpads to reach the enemy's platforms and if you get eliminated, you'll be given a second chance to help your team by defeating enemies in the Ghoulag.

PROP HUNT: MODERN MALL (1679-1165-5282)

The classic hide-and-seek game mode returns and pits the props versus hunters in a shopping centre setting. If you're designated as a prop, you can change into an everyday object that you'd find in a mall, but you ping every 15 seconds so the hunter will have an idea of where you're hiding. If you're discovered, you'll respawn as a hunter to track down remaining props.

ZOMBIENITE (8678-9448-5299)

While Fortnitemares pits you against undead terrors during the Halloween season, Zombienite lets you loose against waves of shambling horrors at any time of the year. You and four friends can drop into one of three maps to do battle – the Backrooms, The House and The Prison. But no matter your destination, you'll have to use your wits to fight off thousands of ghouls to survive!

THE SPACE INSIDE (9836-7381-5978)

Are you smart enough to escape this series of puzzling rooms? Epic Games themselves put this experience together to showcase what Creative 2.0 was capable of now that the Unreal Engine had been woven into the experience. You start off in a creepy empty room, get your hands on a weak torch and must use your wits to solve the puzzles and escape the mysterious facility.

RECLAMATION (1135-0371-8937)

For those Fortnite fans who want a throwback to gaming days of yesteryear, this 8v8 game mode might be the perfect dose of nostalgia. You can pick one of five classic loadouts, each with different weapons and abilities before being thrown on the map to claim and control one of the drill sites, which will give your team points the longer you hold it and fend off the enemies.

JUNGLE SLIDE (9913-8967-3032)

Take a break from gunplay and hop over to Jungle Slide, a parkour marathon that only masters of movement will be able to manoeuvre through. Sprint through the flora of a wild jungle dotted with decrepit ruins and hop, jump and rail-slide across the logs to collect treasure and last as long as possible. You'll need quick fingers and excellent timing to make it all the way to the end.

BUT WAIT – THERE'S MORE!

Turn to page 46 to discover another selection of the best games that the community have built.

BACK TO BASICS: WEAPONS

After over 25 different seasons, it's anyone's guess what weapons will be in rotation during any given season. However, each weapon belongs to a class and if you know the basic strengths and weaknesses of each class, then you'll be able to pick up any firearm and wield it with skill.

MELEE

If, for some reason, you want to bring a swing to a gunfight, grab a melee weapon. You'll be outmatched in most cases, though some options like the Kinetic Blade, which allows you to dash in mid-air, can give you abilities to compensate for this. If worst comes to worst and you're ambushed before you have a gun, you can even fight back with your harvesting tool, but with strictly limited results.

PISTOLS

The baby of the arsenal, pistols are great when you're battling at short or medium distances. They generally have decent reload speed, accuracy and power, but different pistols have different strengths for all of these. A Hand Cannon, for example, is way more powerful than a basic pistol, but won't fire as quickly, while Suppressed Pistols are almost silent, highly accurate but a little weaker.

SMGS

Another option for short or mid-range combat is the submachine gun, otherwise known as an SMG. They sacrifice accuracy for automatic fire so they can be erratic the further away you are from your intended target. They generally have lower damage compared to rifles as well as being less accurate, but models like the Compact SMG has increased damage and Burst SMGs will give you more control.

SHOTGUNS

If accuracy isn't your strong suit, get your hands on a shotgun and unleash a hail of bullets with every pull of the trigger. They're slow to reload and better suited to close combat because of the wide bullet spray, but will do massive damage if you make a good connection. Fully automatic versions like the Tactical Shotgun or Drum Shotgun just feel unfair sometimes ... better make sure they're in your hands.

AMMO STASH

The best gun you can use is one that you have ammo for. There's no point picking up a Legendary sniper rifle if you don't have the ammo to load into it. Make sure you're always picking up more ammo than weapons and you'll be just fine.

ASSAULT RIFLES

The most versatile firearm is the assault rifle, which excels at all ranges, whether aiming down the sights from a distance or firing from the hip at nearby targets. They do tend to lose a bit of accuracy when firing from the hip, and weapons like the Light Machine Gun fire wildly, but there are more variants of the AR than any other gun, so there's always a model out there to compensate for its shortfalls.

BACK TO BASICS: WEAPONS

MARKSMAN RIFLES

If you've got an eagle eye and aim to match, try your hand at a marksman rifle. They usually have powerful scopes that can help you spot targets way across the map and do immense damage on impact, often knocking enemies with one hit. But they're awful at anything but long range because of their terrible hipfire accuracy, so make sure you have a pistol or shotgun in your inventory too.

SNIPER RIFLES

Slightly more versatile than the marksman rifles, sniper rifles also reward players that have good accuracy, but have better rates of fire and a wider pool of options. Shots you fire are subject to other forces, so you might need to compensate for gravity over a long distance, unless you're using a variant like a Rail Gun, which hits exactly where your reticule is aimed.

NADES

Nades, short for grenades, are limited throwable weapons that typically explode, though there are dozens of different effects that the explosions can have beyond mere damage. Cuddle Fish can miss their target, but still jump on them if they're nearby before exploding. The boogie bomb makes anyone in its vicinity dance, while remote explosives are not thrown but planted and ignited by your trigger!

BOWS AND CROSSBOWS

Though they can be a little trickier than other weapons, and getting used to the looping trajectories takes some time, bows and crossbows can be great at mid-range if you can master them. Depending on the bow you're wielding, the arrows and bolts you fire often have secondary damage too, like an explosion or poisonous stink cloud.

LAUNCHERS

If you want to combine the chaos of grenades with the range of assault rifles, rummage through chests until you've secured a launcher. The standard Grenade Launcher sends grenades away in an arc, while Rocket Launchers generally send their warhead off in a straight line. Some launchers, such as the Anvil Rocket Launcher, could even lock onto targets and send a homing explosive!

INVENTIVE ITEMS

Nothing has changed in Fortnite's inventory over the last five years, except they keep adding wilder items to fill your slots with. Let's take a trip down memory lane and look at some items that do battle with your weaponry for prime position in the inventory.

HEALING

A shoo-in for the coveted final slot of your inventory, healing items are a must-have unless your strategy is hide and hope nobody finds you. Bandages heal just 15 health and can stack higher than a Med Kit, which heals for 100, but will only heal you up to a max of 75. The Pizza Party item could be thrown and shared with a squad, with each slice recovering 25 health and shield.

SHIELDS

Another inventory essential are shield items, which come in various shapes and sizes. The common Small Shield Potion is found in stacks of three and applies up to 50 shield points, whereas the shield potion does 50 in a single gulp up to 100. The Shield Keg was a throwable item that sprinkled up to 4 shield points to anyone around the blast radius – enemies included.

RANGED

Not every item involves consuming something you hold in your hands. This collection of ranged items are a halfway-house between weapon and tool with a variety of effects, from unleashing a structure-shredding circular saw to launching health down your duo's throat!

FORAGED ITEMS

You're looting items left, right and centre, but you might often overlook the consumable items that lie on the ground. They're not the most powerful items – in most cases, but they can help you top up health and shields if you're desperate.

APPLE

The basic consumable you'll find littering many a forest, the apple simply restores five health points. Hoover them up, hide away and devour a whole tree's worth.

MUSHROOM

Like the apple, mushrooms are found in dark areas under forest canopies, but get to work on the shield bar instead, adding five points per fungi.

PEPPER

This spicy little veg gives you an extra burst of speed to help you rush away from (or into) a dangerous battle. The effect stacks too, so the more you eat, the faster you get.

BATTLE ITEMS

All items can turn the tide of battle, whether it's topping up health and shields before you assault a base, or a shot from a flare gun that shows you the way to safety. This assortment of clever inventory-hoggers, however, have a particular use when you're looking for eliminations.

DECOY

Just because you're outmatched, it doesn't mean that all hope is lost. With the Decoy, you could outsmart the enemy instead by tossing the item to create a perfect recreation of yourself that runs, shoots and distracts, which allows you to sneak into a better position.

JUNK RIFT

There are very few funnier ways to eliminate an enemy than dropping a load of trash on their head and the Junk Rift allowed you to do just that. Throw the makeshift nade at the ground to open a rift that deposits a huge piece of rubbish directly onto that spot.

RIFT-TO-GO

So the battle's not going your way, you're trapped in the cellar of a house and a whole squad is descending on you with legendary weapons. No worries! Lob the Rift-To-Go to deploy your own personal rift and drop in from the skies above once more. Easy!

PORT-A-FORT

Sometimes building in the middle of a firefight can be a chore – the enemy will only shoot it down after all! Introducing the Port-A-Fort, which magically constructs a metallic bastion right before your eyes. The Port-A-Fortress variant is even bigger and is so useful!

AIR STRIKE

A legendary item that hasn't endured for long in Fortnite because it's just too powerful. You would launch a canister of smoke to mark a blast range, calling in a hail of twenty missiles that could obliterate enemy and building alike.

BOOM BOX

If you wanted a method of destruction that was a bit more pleasing on the ears, you could've opted for the Boom Box. The vibrations from this overpowered ghetto blaster were enough to shake the foundations of buildings and destroy them in seconds.

FISHING ITEMS

Aquatic creatures have been a part of Fortnite since Chapter 2 and even though they took a well-deserved break during Fortnite OG, they've been an important part of the game ever since. If you could get your hands on a Fishing Rod (or the Pro version) or a Harpoon, which acted more like a gun, you could cast off and catch one of the marvellous marine animals below.

FLOPPER

The OG healing fish, the Flopper was one of the first to swim the waters of the island and was very useful for healing up to 40 health in a flash – much better than bandages.

HOP FLOPPER

When the Flopper population expanded in Chapter 2, Season 4, Hop Floppers were highly sought-after for their ability to reduce a player's gravity!

JELLYFISH

Sometimes it's nice to share your best items, but the Jellyfish allowed you to have your cake and eat it. Consuming it would restore 20 health to you and everyone around you!

MIDAS FLOPPER

Another addition in Chapter 2, Season 4, the Midas Flopper was a god-tier catch. Not only did it heal you, but it also upgraded everything in your inventory to Legendary rarity!

SMALL FRY

The most common haul when you're out fishing, the Small Fry operate exactly the same as bandages, giving you 25 health up to a maximum of 75.

RIFT FISH

Rift-To-Gos are handy when you're in a tough spot, but what if you also got a little bit of healing when you used one? The Rift Fish creates a similar rift and restores 15 health!

SHADOW FLOPPER

Chapter 2, Season 8 brought a brand new version of the Flopper that could restore health but also turn you into a shadow, making you almost invisible for a while.

MISCELLANEOUS ITEMS

So you can heal, land a catch and gain the edge in battle with the correct selection of items, but their utility doesn't stop there. Here are some other items that defy classification, but are incredibly useful nonetheless.

GAS CAN

If you're planning on jumping in one of Fortnite's vehicles, then having a Gas Can among your items is a necessity. You wouldn't want your Choppa to droppa out of the sky would you? If you throw a Gas Can and attack it, it will explode too, just in case you need a makeshift explosive at short notice.

BUSH

There's nothing special about this bush other than the fact that you can wear it! Stay completely still and you'll blend in with the surroundings – providing you're in a leafy forest or garden and not the bedroom of a busy building!

OFF-ROAD TIRES

Cars can struggle when they're not driving on smooth surfaces like roads, so if you can get your hands on the Off-Road Tires vehicle mod, you can make them faster on trickier terrain. The giant wheels also have more health than regular tyres, so it will take enemies longer to shoot out your wheels.

COW CATCHER

The Cow Catcher was a vehicle mod that you could attach to the grill of your car to make them more powerful, hitting enemies for extra damage if you run through them. Not only that, it had 800 health, which provided an extra layer of protection to your car ... as long as enemies were shooting the front of the vehicle of course.

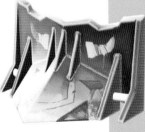

DAMAGE TRAP

There once was a time when traps like the Damage Trap – a pressure-activated spiky surface – were the bane of players everywhere. You'd wander into a seemingly empty building chasing the hum of a loot chest, only to be instantly impaled and lose half your health. Luckily, they've been cast off the island since Chapter 2, Season 2.

STORM FLIP

At the end of the first chapter, the Storm Flip was an excellent way of evading the encroaching storm. If you were racing to get inside the storm circle, you could use the Storm Flip to create a sphere of safety as you rushed towards the safe zone. However, if you were in the safe haven inside the storm, it would create a damaging mini-storm!

GETTING AROUND

Now that sprinting, sliding and mantling have been added to Fortnite, travelling by foot is a great way to navigate the island. But it's not the only way. If you prefer more speed and style, hop in or on one of Fortnite's many modes of transportation. The most common vehicles on the island are those that cover the ground, ranging from the humble Shopping Cart to the way-over-the-top Armoured Battle Bus!

BY LAND

SHOPPING CART

If you still want to get exercise in while you're driving, the Shopping Cart does require one person to push and move it. A second player can sit in the cart itself and shoot at enemies as you go. It's good fun but slow, unless you're going down a hill ...

DRIFTBOARD

Landing in Season 7 of the first Chapter, the Driftboard was a game-changer. Not only did it have a boost function that let you pull off cool tricks while you grabbed some air, but you could also shoot, throw nades and heal while you were travelling at epic top speeds!

TITAN TANK

When the war between the Imagined Order and The Seven was heating up, they deployed the tanks! This slow-moving beast trundled along the battlefield and unleashed its cannon at targets big and small. It was excellent at destroying structures.

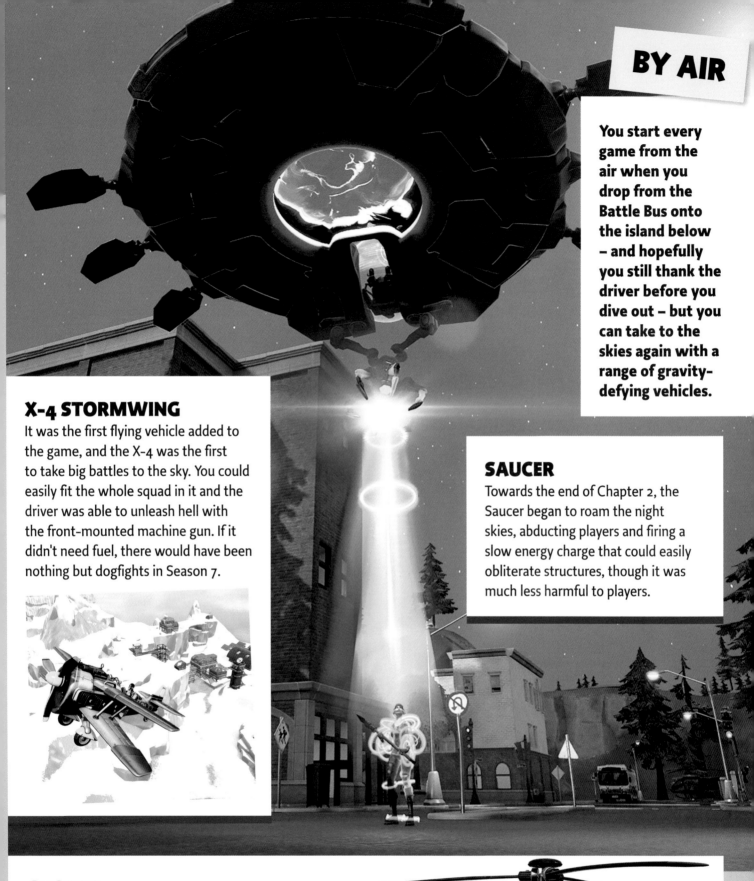

You start every game from the air when you drop from the Battle Bus onto the island below – and hopefully you still thank the driver before you dive out – but you can take to the skies again with a range of gravity-defying vehicles.

X-4 STORMWING

It was the first flying vehicle added to the game, and the X-4 was the first to take big battles to the sky. You could easily fit the whole squad in it and the driver was able to unleash hell with the front-mounted machine gun. If it didn't need fuel, there would have been nothing but dogfights in Season 7.

SAUCER

Towards the end of Chapter 2, the Saucer began to roam the night skies, abducting players and firing a slow energy charge that could easily obliterate structures, though it was much less harmful to players.

CHOPPA

For those that needed a bit more stability when they're sniping from the clouds, the Choppa's ability to hover really gave them a boost. It was a little more fragile than the X-4 but almost as fast, which made it great for escaping the storm with your squad.

GETTING AROUND

Believe it or not, Fortnite hasn't always had water! Before Chapter 2 arrived, there were no rivers or lakes (except shallow ones like Loot Lake), no boats, no fishing and certainly no swimming. But when water started to flow, the players needed ways to get around on it.

MOTORBOAT

As players got familiar with traversing the water that flooded the island in Chapter 2, boats became the hot vehicle to have. They could shoot missiles that annihilated structures and could also ride out onto the land ... although that would damage the boat!!

SURFBOARD

This one is only available in Creative mode, but if the Loot Shark gave you a taste for riding the waves, hop on a surfboard and carve through the water. It has the same feel as riding a Driftboard on land and even has the same boost ability.

LOOT SHARK

This is one for the braver sailors. If you could hunt down a Loot Shark and hook it with a rod, you could control the treasure-hungry predator like any other vehicle. It even had a boost.
However, it could also take half your health with a single bite. Worth the risk? Always!

We've covered land, sea and air, so what more can there be to cover? Well some of the ways to get around in Fortnite are so unconventional, so downright odd, that they need their own special category. Let's look at the weirdest ways to make moves around the island.

PIRATE CANNON

In the swashbuckling eighth season, the Pirate Cannon arrived with a boom. They were found in Lazy Lagoon and could either shoot cannonballs at enemies, or you could load yourself into the chamber and fire yourself across the map. Mad!

BY OTHER MEANS

THE BALLER

If you thought players using a Grappler to evade you were nimble ninjas, the good folks at Epic attached one to a super-strong hamster ball. Only one player could fit inside, but could use the grappler to manoeuvre around. Combined with the boost ability, it was deadly ball-bouncing chaos.

B.R.U.T.E.

Technically this counts as travelling by land, but when you and a buddy hop into the B.R.U.T.E., it feels like so much more. It was generally slow, but the driver could use dash and stomp attacks, while the gunner player fired off rockets and shotguns simultaneously. Epic!

SUIT UP

The best part of the Battle Pass that drops every season is undoubtedly the collection of creative skins, whether it's battle-hardened combat veterans, anthropomorphic bananas or crossovers from your favourite films. Let's look at the best skins from Fortnite's first four chapters.

FISHSTICK

This hapless looking fish could lull your enemies into a false sense of security. Its silly hat, gormless expression and ill-fitting onesie look a little unusual, but you can upgrade it to one of the cooler VR goggle-wearing or wicked pirate variants.

GUILD

If you need an explorer who's ready for any adventure then Guild is your man. He's got a grappling hook, a trusty knife and ... a pen. If it's cold outside, you can switch to his Winter Hunter variant, which has a woolly jumper instead of a short tee.

MANCAKE

Covered with butter bandoliers and topped with a delicious dripping syrup, this sweet shot goes by Mancake. He became a fan favourite when he dropped in Chapter 2 and has six awesome variants, including the Western-inspired The Cake With No Name.

SIONA

You can't get into the stratosphere from the Island, but that hasn't stopped the cosmic queen Siona dropping by in her spacefaring garb. She's part of the Ancient Voyager set, which also includes Deo, who dropped a season later, but both can choose whether to don their helmet or not!

TRACY TROUBLE

A reward for subscribing to the Fortnite Crew feature, Tracy Trouble was released as an exclusive epic skin at the start of Chapter 3. With a striking hot pink and black outfit and multicoloured hair, she's sure to cause a riotous scene on the island.

FISH THICC

Available from the Chapter 4, Season 4 Battle Pass, Fish Thicc is on a whole new scale compared to the teensy Fishstick. The buff swimmer is rippling with muscles under his low-slung tank top, but still has those spines bulging through his trousers.

LIL SPLIT

One of the combo skins that dropped in Season OG, Lil Split is a mix of fan-favourite skins Peely and Lil Whip. This deliciously frosty banana sports a stylish and tasty aviator jacket!

PEELY'S ADVENTURES

Including Lil Split, there are over ten different versions of Peely skins, from the OG banana and the spooky Peely Bone, which shows the fruit's unconventional skeleton.

RENEGADE LYNX

Blending the aviation themes of Renegade Raider and the feline qualities of Lynx, Renegade Lynx is another awesome Season OG combo. The goggles and flight hat now sport cat ears and she still has her trusty mask to throw on if that's not enough to protect her.

SHIMMERDUSK

It takes a brave person to stand against the mighty vampire Kado Thorne. The grey fae Shimmerdusk is one of them. The huntress hunts down monsters of the night across time, space and even dimensions, and looks super cool as she does it.

SUIT UP

MAGNUS

As one of the OG Vikings available in Season 5 (along with Huntress), you might not have seen Magnus around much recently. Who knows why he fell out of favour though, with his awesome intimidating helmet, spiky gauntlets and an immaculately plaited beard. What a terror!

HAXSAUR

When ferocious dinosaurs and complex computations are combined, you end up with something like Haxsaur, a prehistoric mechanical marvel. He sports a casual hoody to tamper the fear factor a little, but still instils fear on the battlefield.

BOXER

You were expecting a buff fighting guy, right? Sorry to disappoint, but Boxer is literally just a man wearing boxes. Enemies will be perplexed as a stack of storage equipment charges them on the island, but surely cardboard doesn't offer much protection ...

RENEGADE SHADOW

Once known to be a lone wolf that lurked in the dark corners of the map, this super-cool super-spy became something of a heist expert when Chapter 4 was released. He always wears his trademark fur-collared coat, but his tactical mask and goggles are optional.

SPECTRA KNIGHT

The flagship skin from Season OG's Battle Pass, and the only one that doesn't seem to be a combination of previous skins. This slick knight has a customisable colour scheme and armour pattern, as well as four additional helmets that could be unlocked by ranking up the BP.

DOUBLE AGENT HUSH

It's already tricky to work out who the good guys and bad guys are, without throwing double agents into the mix. Sigh. At least Double Agent Hush has been around since Chapter 2, Season 3, so you're used to the double-crossing now, right?

DUMMY

This bright-yellow individual is done taking the hits in crash tests of its safety-testing past and has switched to dishing out damage instead. It has a carbon fibre variant too, which should make it a little more durable and a lot more modern!

SIREN

Having the use of one eye doesn't seem to diminish Siren's prowess on the battlefield one bit. This slick hitwoman has one of the best variants in the game – Noir – which makes her look like she's from a classic black-and-white spy thriller. We would be terrified seeing her in battle!

OMEGAROK

What happens when you combine the tech of a sinister cyber-ninja and the sheer power of a godlike viking? Omegarok happens. It's a combination of the Omega and Ragnarok skins, and has Norse power flowing through its sleek black body armour.

RUBY

This street-smart cool cat has been dominating the battlefield since Season X. Not surprisingly given her name, Ruby is easy to spot in her red threads, though her variants mix it up if you want to become a multicoloured hero.

CREATIVE MODE MAPS 2

Creative 2.0 made it possible to create any kind of game in Fortnite, not just shooters. Take a look at these inventive minigames and you'll see just how flexible the system is, all without needing to frantically hoover up the best shotguns.

FORTNITE FUNLAND (2057-3742-0636)

Sometimes you need to take a break from the grind of Battle Royale, so Fortnite Funland is the perfect place to visit for a spot of rest and relaxation. You can ride epic rollercoasters, brave the drop tower and see the sights on a Ferris wheel, but that's not to say there isn't room for a bit of competition. The amusement park is full of minigames like Cosmic Frisby Frenzy too!

TRUCK PURSUIT (7832-3964-5638)

Buckle up because you're in for a bumpy ride! You'll even be put in the driving seat of a car or a truck on a wild island full of massive ramps and hidden shortcuts. Cars must avoid being hit by the truck while they zoom around, while the truck driver must try and hit everyone within the allotted time. Be careful how fast you're driving though, because if you fall off the edge, you're eliminated!

50 FASHION SHOW (3589-2124-6433)

Now for something completely different. The island has long been a home for showing off the latest skins, gliders and other accessories, but now players can don their greatest looks and strut down the catwalk to see if others love their style. Up to 50 players will vote on a variety of different themes across three rounds. Do you have the style skills to come out on top?

FOREST GUARDIAN   (0348-4483-3263)

This bewitching adventure drops you in a mysterious world inhabitated by a gigantic guardian. Armed with just a sword, you must take down the guardian's minions and survive long enough to see the fantastical sight. It's a very short game that was made by Epic to show off the boosted visuals that they could now include in their Creative minigames.

TEDDY   (6890-1483-5306)

If you're a fan of frights, Teddy might just be the minigame that you're looking for. It's an asymmetrical horror game, which means that six survivors must do their best to escape a single player that takes the role of Teddy. Survivors must try to find the keys to escape a handful of levels before Teddy manageds to hunt them down. Who will come out on top?

COLOR SWITCH   (1415-7321-0392)

Grab your friends and drop into Color Switch, a frantic party game that tasks you with outlasting the other competitors by quickly hopping to the correct colour platform. If you don't make it in time, your platform will fall away beneath you and you'll be eliminated. But don't worry, there are even minigames to play, like kart races and parkour, while you wait for the next round.

COMPLETE THE LOOK

There are loads of ways to customise the way you play and create a look that will light up the island. A strong look can also strike fear into your enemies. On these pages, we'll look at all the different items and options available to you in Fortnite!

RENEGADE RUSTCAT

If it wasn't for the cute cat ears that top this back bling, the bullet-lined rusty sphere might look like something dangerous that you'd much rather avoid than cause harm to yourself!

RAPTOR SATCHEL

You'll never be more prepared for the battlefield than when you're sporting the Raptor Satchel, complete with flask, spade and so much roarsome equipment hidden inside.

BACK BLING

JONES' FIELD PACK

Stock up like one of Fortnite's favourite characters, Agent Jones, with this super-stuffed backpack. There are variants from different expeditions that add more to the pack too!

PEELY WHIP

As if there aren't enough Peelys running around the island, you can now carry a baby version of the loveable banana right on your back!

APOCALYPSE SHROUD

If you're more the type to let your actions do the talking, grab this understated cape from your locker. It's simple and angular, except for the small glowing mech at the top. Totally terrific!

SHADOW STALKER

Sometimes relying on gravity and air resistance isn't enough. The Shadow Stalker employs two mini rockets to safely guide you to a smooth landing.

SUNDAE GLIDER

Made from sugar, spice and all things nice, the Sundae Glider is an ice-cream creation that is bound to hit the spot. Let's hope that wafers float well ...

RAIDER'S WAYFARER

Available in base and Dark Storm variants, the Raider's Wayfarer lets you surf to the island on a futuristic three-pronged hoverboard shuttle!

CHAIN SURFER

It's a good thing that you can only use this while you're dropping, because that chain would cause more chaos than Kevin the Cube if it touched the ground.

GLIDERS

FROSTBURN

An updated version of the incredible Frostwing glider that blends in the tech style of the Terminus, Frostburn will strike fear into any foe that sees you!

HARVESTING TOOLS

NOGGIN

As if Dummy hasn't been through enough already, now someone's put its head on the end of an axe! Sorry buddy, but those materials need to be harvested ... you don't mind, do you?

SPECTRA SLASHER

An elegant combination of axe and scythe, the crystalline Spectra Slasher is a classy harvesting tool that perfectly suits the Spectra Knight skin.

SCRATCHMARK SHREDDER

The glowing claw-scratched blade of this pickaxe seems as sturdy as any other despite suffering what looks like some sort of feline attack ...

NANNER BASHERS

Sometimes it's amazing what you can use to bash in wood, stone and metal. This pair of popsicles seem like they'd splat when you swing them, but they certainly do the job.

WINTER'S ONSLAUGHT

If you need a bit of extra power behind your swings, then Winter's Onslaught is the tool for you. It has an ethereal engine on its head that seems to make every swing a little stronger.

COMPLETE THE LOOK

RAIDER'S RETURN

Coat your weapons in Raider's Return to give them a metallic sheen and a customised two-coloured finish. Super slick!

GLITTER N' GRIM

Contrast the sparkly golden lining with the bleak dark patterns and you've got a skin that will suit whatever mood you find yourself in.

JUST DESSERTS

Made with sprinkles and wafers, the Just Desserts wrap is perfect for securing the sweetest of victories. If you can keep your belly from rumbling that is. So tasty!

CUBEFALL

It's been a long time since the Cubes wreaked havoc on the island, but let everyone know you'll never forget with this pair of violet cubic contrails.

SPECTRAKINETIC

Give your weapons and vehicles a classy minimalist look by shrouding them in the Spectrakinetic wrap, with its smooth white base and golden patterns.

FINAL HARBINGER

If you pair this wrap with the Omegarok skin, then the glowing colour of the skin will match the one on your weapons and vehicles. Complete the set!

SHARDFALL

It must be chilly dropping at such a great height from the Battle Bus and now it's confirmed, as Shardfall sends fragments of ice-like shards trailing behind you.

RAGE'N'ROCK

Channel your inner Viking as you fall by grabbing hold of the thick, glowing chains in the Rage'n'Rock contrail. Just make sure you let go to pull out your trusty glider.

KNIGHT'S HONOR

Emblazon Spectra Knight in all her glory on any surface you see fit. The brave heroine is shown brandishing a shield, with her fist set to strike anyone within range.

AURORAL ARC

Channel the wonder of the Northern Lights and let the auroras leave a dazzling display behind you. The Auroral Arc may be hypnotic enough to distract your landing enemies.

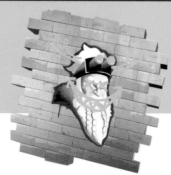

NAUGHTY OR NICE

You know it's that type of year when Sgt. Winter begins to appear everywhere, but someone seems to have sprayed all over this handsome portrait. He's going to be angry!

SPLIT HAPPENS

Life advice from Fortnite's latest Peely incarnation is the perfect piece to emblazon on the buildings of the island as you gloat over your latest win.

DESSERT DROPPER

Serve up a treat to anyone that's trailing behind you with the Dessert Dropper. It sends out streams of ice cream and scatterings of delicious toppings on your descent.

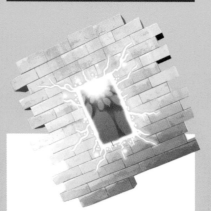

RIFT-STERPIECE

It's not uncommon to see a rift open up around the island, so trick your enemies into thinking they can visit another world with this rifty canvas.

BOOGIE

Take it back to the old skool with some classic graffiti lettering. You can use it to mark your territory or just inform any enemies that you have a stack of Boogie Bombs ready.

THE GOOD GUYS

The island has brought together heroes, villains and organisations from different realities and timelines, so you might need a hand working out who's friend and who's foe. Let's meet some of the benevolent heroes and factions that seek to keep the island safe and sound.

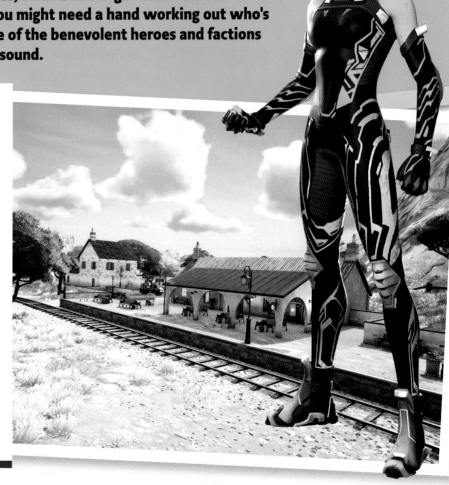

THE SEVEN

This septuplet of heroes – and former heroes – is the driving force of good on the Island. The group is comprised of seven individuals (of course) who stand against the evil Imagined Order. One of it's members, The Visitor, crashed down on the island in Season 3, launched a rocket to create several rifts and eventually led to The End in Season X. Their remaining members reside in Sanctuary, which was revealed on the island in Chapter 3, but today they're all missing or deceased, so you have to continue their good work and fight the good fight.

PEACE SYNDICATE

Also known as just The Syndicate, this motley crew originates from the same timeline as MEGA City. Though they're tasked with upholding peace, they often use shady means and count many criminals among their ranks. After assisting The Seven in taking down the Imagined Order, they took over Cuddle Cruisers in Chapter 3, Season 3 and transformed it into their new headquarters, Syndicate Shoals. When MEGA City dropped from a rift in the second season of Chapter 4, members Evie and Thunder began hunting down a saboteur from The Last Reality ...

THE ANCIENTS

A timeless race with mastery over rifts, though they seem to have disappeared from the island entirely. However, they've left behind ruins in the jungle areas of the island, filled with undecipherable runes that may leave clues about how to use the rifts – as well as lots of incredible technology like the Kinetic Boomerang. Some myths suggest that the Ancients went into hiding when Kado Thorne came to power.

THE EXPLORERS

A mish-mash of inquisitive folks hailing from factions across the good-to-evil spectrum, the Explorers have just one aim – to unravel the mysteries left behind by The Ancients. They're led by the reformed Doctor Slone, who defected from the Imagined Order when she was trapped in the jungle during the Fracture. They include Trace and Era among their ranks – the latter has access to all the amazing memories of her ancestors to help the cause.

THE HEIST CREW

Assembled by the master thief Nolan Chance, The Heist Crew were an informal organisation that hoped to get their hands on Kado Thorne's time machine to regain control of the time shenanigans plaguing the island. They launched an infiltration on Thorne's Eclipsed Estate with the help of vampire-hunters The High Stakes Club, which eventually landed them the time machine, but it was locked on a course five years in the past.

SOLID DEFENCE

Most players in Battle Royale will race around collecting weapons, hunting down enemies and shooting o[...]
sight, so you might need to counter that with some defensive strategies from time to time. Let's look at
how you can survive as long as possible by battening down the hatches.

NINJA TACTICS

If you want to be super smart, or you're just a little scared of being eliminated early, then you could adopt a stealthy approach to the match. You can hide if enemies are nearby, use items to create distractions elsewhere and loot weapons from the ground before you risk silencing the notable hum of a treasure chest. When you're fully kitted out, you can then go on the offensive.

BUILD, BUILD, BUILD

It doesn't matter whether you're facing off against a noob or a pro, the person who can throw up a wall to peek from will always have the advantage. If you don't build, you're going to struggle in battles – unless you're playing Zero Build, of course. Get used to quickly putting up walls when you're being shot at or constructing ramps and 1x1s to keep the enemy guessing where you are.

ELEVATED ADVANTAGE

If you're bunkering down to wait for enemies, pick a spot on top of a cliff or tall building. Not only will you be able to see approaching opponents for miles around, but you'll also be harder to reach and have the upper hand if the enemy starts firing at you. Couple this with a sniper rifle and you'll be as safe as houses until the storm circle rolls in.

EAR ME NOW

Having eyes over a huge area of the map is going to keep you a step ahead of the competition, but what you hear is just as important as what you see. Shots firing will give you an idea of where at least a couple of enemies are, and if you're hunkered down in a defensive position, you'll want to listen out for approaching footsteps creeping up on you ...

TURN TAIL

Sometimes, despite your best-laid plans and some superb shooting, it can look like your opponents are going to finish you off. If you get the chance, there's no shame in escaping as quickly as you possibly can. You'll get the chance to heal, collect up more ammo, items and better weapons, then lie in wait to exact your revenge. Never be afraid to run!

ALL-OUT ATTACK

If you drop in an area full of people, you'll need to start on the front foot and begin racking up the eliminations before you're sent packing from the island. These offensive tactics will help you inch closer to the all-important Victory Royale.

STAY MOBILE

If you want to be the last person standing, you need to stay on the move. Not only will this allow you to round up the best weapons and plenty of ammo, but it will mean you see more enemies along your travels. It's much easier to execute your best strategy in a firefight within a wide open map than waiting until you're squished into the the storm circle's final stages with your adversaries.

THE BEST WEAPON

... isn't a weapon at all – it's your building skills. If you're facing off in a 1v1, the enemy is likely going to try to build their way out of trouble, so you need to match those efforts. Ramping up will give you a height advantage if you're fast enough, but editing their builds to have windows and doors will also help you get your shots off on the enemy when they don't expect it.

CHANNEL THE STORM

When the storm circle shrinks, remaining players will race to get back inside the safe zone. Well, it would be safe if you weren't waiting to pick them off. If you have a good position inside the safe zone already, watch the edge of the circle for incoming players and eliminate them one by one. Because they're outside the circle, they're unlikely to try building their way out of trouble too!

EQUIP WISELY

You never know when you're going to discover an enemy sneaking up on you, or get nailed by a sniper shot from afar, so it's important to keep different weapon ranges in your hotbar. Shotguns and pistols are great for close encounters and assault or sniper rifles are perfect for long distances. Don't worry if you're bad with certain weapons, it's just important to have the right tools – you're not going to defeat a sniper with a pistol, are you?

USE BURSTS

While weapons like the Burst Assault Rifle rotates in and out of the vault, you can still apply its principles to any automatic weapon. If you just spray and pray, you're likely to lose track of a target and waste ammo, so shoot a couple at a time, readjust your aim then fire off another couple of shots. Enemies aren't going to stand around and make themselves an easy target!

THE BAD GUYS

Many evils have plagued the island over the last five years, all of them with their own private machinations for moulding it as they see fit. Here's a who's-who of Fortnite's antagonists so you know exactly who to be on the lookout for.

IMAGINED ORDER

You may know it as The Order or IO, but the big bad of the island is Geno's malevolent organisation that seeks to maintain balance in the Omniverse ... which normally means bad things for the island's residents. Geno gained control over The Zero Point long ago and used it to access infinite realities, rinsing each of their knowledge and power. IO is responsible for unleashing The Devourer on the island, as well as The Zero Point, which swallowed up the island before The Seven could reconstruct it.

THE LAST REALITY

If controlling and pillaging all realities wasn't bad enough, then The Last Reality takes IO's plans a step further – they want to end all other realities and return the Omniverse to nothingness! They have the power to cross realities too, and their original leader The Cube King, escaped when he found out that his cubes were evil. He was captured by IO but rescued by The Seven, where he became The Origin, the seventh member of the faction. However, the Cube Queen took his place and sent cubes to the island to wreak havoc over the land.

ECLIPSE

Some villains hide right in plain sight. Eclipse posed as estate agents, but this is just a front for a clandestine organisation led by the vampire Kado Thorne, who is sucking the resources from the island. In Chapter 4, Season 4, beneath the scarlet skies, Thorne holed up in the Eclipsed Estate as The Heist Crew attempted to steal his riches from him, as well as a mysterious time machine, but he deployed his lieutenants, known as Dealers to stop them in their tracks.

OATHBOUND

Occupying the grey area between good and evil, the Oathbound faction was created by Geno a long time ago, but he abandoned them when he formed The Imagined Order. They went on to make their home in The Citadel, which was then pulled into the Island at the beginning of Chapter 4. There was a dark entity haunting The Citadel, so the rift wardens of the kingdom attempted to create a rift gate. Their risky plan was to hunt down the entity, but it backfired and created a sideways rift in the sky.

CREATIVE MODE MAPS 3

It's time for our final entry on the most incredible games from the Creative 2.0 world. Whether you want to practise your movement, survive for longer on an even more dangerous island or even run your own version of Fortnite, these codes will keep you entertained for hours!

FORT WHO? (5794-2200-8636)

Pit your wits against an opponent in a guessing game featuring some of Fortnite's most famous characters. Players need to work out which character their opponent has chosen by asking questions to eliminate a board full of suspects (with a sniper rifle!) and land on the correct character. The first to work out who the other player actually chose is the winner.

FORTNITE TYCOON (5483-0156-1022)

Ever thought how hard the devs at Epic work to keep your favourite game running? Well now you've got the chance to jump in their shoes and maintain your own version of Fortnite, in competition with three other players doing the same thing. Green buttons upgrade your studio, while the blue ones update the game, which you can see being built up in real time!

TOWER DEFENSE: SWISSCOM HERO CITY (1359-7035-5992)

Team up with a fellow citizen to defend the futuristic metropolis from an army of robotic bugs that are invading along a winding road. Nice of them to follow a path at least! For every bug you defeat, you'll receive coins that you can spend to buy or upgrade towers that attack the enemy or give you more gold. But let too many bugs through and it's game over for you and the city!

THE ONLY WAY IS UP! (6342-0361-0172)

One-shot games, where a single wrong move will send you crashing back to the beginning of the WHOLE GAME, have become all the rage in recent years. The Only Way Is Up! challenges you to leap to the top of a sprawling pile of Fortnite debris that's floating in the air. But be careful ... one step out of place and you'll plummet back to the ground.

CARKOUR (4673-7855-8449)

Why is all the parkour fun taking place on foot? Exactly the question that the Carkour creator teadoh must have been asking when they came up with this bonkers vehicle-based obstacle course. Hop in a truck and make your way along the various platforms, which range from regular roads and looping ramps to spinning drums and overturned buses!

FORESTZ: ZOMBIE ISLAND (3422-8734-7108)

If you thought surviving on the island for half an hour was difficult, then Forestz: Zombie Island will give you food for thought. Not only do you need to outlast other players, but also hordes of zombies and wild animals. You can forage for weapons, fish for food and build like in the core game, but you've also got things like hunger to keep an eye on, too!

EXPRESS YOURSELF

There are hundreds of emotes now available in the game, ranging from celebrations and dances to funny reactions and cocky gloats. Whatever you want to say in Fortnite, it's best said with one of these ingenious animations.

DICE ROLL

Are you feeling lucky? Well grab the dice, give it a blow and roll it to see how your fortunes are going to play out. This chance emote is part of the Maverick Mastermind set, which includes Mr Lucky himself, Nolan Chance.

SPRINGY

Movement is important in Fortnite – quicker targets are harder to hit after all. But you can't move any quicker than when showing off Springy, which is an excellent exercise in jumping, spinning and hopping on the spot.

FLASHBACK BREAKDOWN

A tribute to some of the best emotes throughout the years, Flashback Breakdown was released as part of the Season OG Battle Pass and included moves from much-loved emotes of yesteryear including Ride the Pony, The Worm and Work It Out.

BOOMIN'

If you need a bit of background music as you enter the final stages of the storm, bust out Boomin'. You'll throw a boombox on your shoulder and blast out a thundering rock song that will charge you up for the final stand.

GENTLEMAN'S DAB

Dabbing can be so uncouth, especially when everyone is overusing it. Add a little bit of class to your showboating by opting for the much more pleasant Gentleman's Dab, which adds in a courteous and classy bow to proceedings.

CLEAN SWEEP

If you've taken out an enemy and all they've dropped is basic common loot, nobody's going to pick it up. Be a responsible islander and throw out the Clean Sweep, which will (try to) brush away the useless rubbish.

DANCE MOVES

The OG emote that literally EVERYBODY was using in the very first season, Dance Moves is still a popular choice in the emote slots to this day. With a short span and the slickest steps, it will probably never go out of fashion.

I LIKE TO MOVE IT

And who doesn't? This series of arm-swinging, toe-tapping, head-bobbing skills has been paraded around the island since the first season of Chapter 3. In fact, it seems that people really LOVED to move it.

DO THE 'SPLIT

An emote that complements the infectious song 'Welcome to the Split Show', Do The 'Split is a coordinated dance that pays tribute to the delicious outfit. It has similar vibes to Drippin' Flavour, which was released alongside the Lil Whip skin.

EXPRESS YOURSELF

LIL ROVER

Sit back and relax as this small space buggy takes you on an expedition around the island. There's not much room so you may get cramp if you stay on for too long, and the beeps and bloops may give your position away quite easily!

DROP THE BASS

Get the squad bumping when you Drop the Bass! Magic up a set of floating DJ decks in front of you, get your team hyped for the battle and then drop the bass to get the party started. You'll need to stop raving to shoot, unfortunately.

REGAL WAVE

Since Season 6 of Fortnite, you've been able to lord it over your loyal subjects and greet them with the Regal Wave. The classy, barely moving hand will be well-rested when it comes time to pick up your shotty.

DOZE DAB

The dab has been a staple of Fortnite ever since the first chapter, but the latest variant of the emote craze ends with a neatly timed nap in the crook of the dabbing elbow. It has the opposite energy of the Infinite Dab, which goes on forever!

BOLD STANCE

Bold is certainly one word for it. Others could include unusual, odd, and also 'what the heck?'. If you want to show that you don't care what anyone thinks, use this one-sided jiggling emote to really let them know.

ZANY

This infectious stomping routine has been a mainstay of the island since its release in Season 4 and millions have taken a walk on the weird side with it. It's perfect to pair with the sillier skins in the game to maximise the zaniness.

KICK BACK

Some people take the game too seriously with all their frantic looting, shooting and building. Take a bit of time out with the Kick Back, which lets you rest on a simple lawn chair as the chaos unfurls before you.

LIL' LONGBOAT

Show your enemies the power you have on the battlefield by summoning a tiny longboat manned by minuscule Vikings beneath your feet. They're not rowing fast enough to match your running speed though, so you may need to make them work a little harder ...

AIR HORN

Whether you want to show your support for your duo's first kill, scare the jeepers out of an unsuspecting enemy or draw every foe from near and far to your position, the klaxon-like air horn is the multi-purpose emote for the job.

SHADOW BOXER

There's no pulling your punches with the Shadow Boxer. There's no need, because there's no enemy – it's just you versus the air. At least you're practising your ducks, dodges and weaves though. They might be handy later on!

BOOT CAMP

If we've learnt anything from looking at the best bits from seasons past, it's that the game is always changing, whether it's the weapons, items or the very map itself. The only thing that won't change is you, so make sure that you stay on top of these skills and grab the Victory Royale.

AIM

No matter what device you're using to play Fortnite, and no matter how good you are at building, eventually it's going to come down to who's the best shot in the final two. Every weapon is different, so always practise with each one in Creative or one of the community maps. Just line up some targets and make sure you're hitting your shots.

MOVEMENT

With the addition of sprinting and mantling, the island of Fortnite became an even greater parkour playground. Spend some time on the map testing out your sprints and slides, determining how quickly you can switch your weapon out and aim, and seeing how high you can reach by climbing the outside of structures, just in case you need to later.

DROPPING

If you can master the drop from the Battle Bus, you'll always be the first to your chosen location. Check the flight path before you set off and mark where you want to land. If it's right below the Battle Bus, make sure to tilt forward and speed up to get there first. If it's far away, drop at an angle, keeping your marker just visible between your legs.

BUILDING

Unless you're playing Zero Build, you're going to need to throw up structures quickly, so practise, practise, practise! Run drills like ramping to reach high positions, waterfalls to place floors from high places and prevent fall damage, and 'crank 90s' to quickly make safe structures consisting of two walls and a ramp, repeatedly built on top of each other.

EDITING

Once you're a pro at building, your next port of call will be editing. Get used to the controls and how to quickly scroll to your favourite edits, like windows to shoot through and doors to enter other structures. Stand in a 1x1 structure of walls and choose a different pattern of edits so they become second nature.

EXPLORING

Keep a curious nature as you battle. The map changes so often and you should take every opportunity to see new parts with each update. You can choose where to drop, but the storm will force you to places that your enemies might know better than you, giving them the upper hand.

LOADOUT

Having to fiddle about with your inventory while you can hear oncoming steps is not ideal, so make sure you've set up your presets so that you can hoover up all the loot and have it in a familiar slot. All you have to worry about is picking up upgrades when your inventory is full and memorising your slots.

GAMECEPTION

Throughout these pages, you've seen dozens of game modes and minigames that you and the rest of the community love, made within Fortnite itself! If you want to get involved and have a go at creating your own, hop into Creative Mode, the workshop to bring your game ideas to life.

HUB

When you first enter Creative mode, you'll be taken to you own personal hub, where you'll see rifts to all of your created islands. If you haven't used Creative yet, interact with the console and select Create New. This will take you to the Select Type screen, where you can choose from a basic island shape or templates for different game modes.

LAND HO

Once you've created your island in the hub, jump through the rift to your island and you'll drop in. You can explore the island to see what you've got to work with, or interact with the different features if you used a template. You can even give the game mode a quick try if the template is ready to be played by others.

MY ISLAND

Now it's time to start setting up your game. Navigate to the menu and select My Island and you'll bring up a screen full of options to change the way games are played on this island. You can alter the team size, whether you respawn infinitely or die just once and environment options like whether there's fog or heavy environment destruction.

INVENTORY

Cycle along to Creative and you'll see every building, object, weapon and item that's ever graced the main Battle Royale island, as well as a few secret developer options. You can scroll through and fill your eight inventory slots with stuff that you want to place in your brand new island. Don't worry if you want to add more than that, you can always alter your inventory later.

PREFABS

Populating a ginormous island can take time – that's why Epic has a whole development team to do it! However, they've also given you a way to cut corners: prefabs. These are giant structures, often composed of many buildings, such as The Citadel's castle ramparts and other iconic buildings you've probably battled on. Use as many of these as you can to create a broad design before fine-tuning the details.

TO THE SKY

Navigating your ever-growing build can get a bit complicated after a while, so double tap the jump button to fly around your map, passing through objects as you go.

LOOT DROP

When you've built your world and the structures that will feature in your game mode, it's time to add the weapons and items. Move to the place that you want to put the item, then press drop and it'll appear at your feet. You can also add sets of items to chests or loot llamas and drop them on the map instead so you have treasure to find.

WE'VE REACHED THE END OF OUR JOURNEY ... FOR NOW.

Remember that the fight for Victory Royale is relentless. Fortnite is continually changing, updating, improving and expanding. Who knows what will happen next on the island? The only thing you can be assured of is that you won't want to miss a moment of the action.

Keep loading up, keep dropping from the Battle Bus and keep learning what it takes to be the best that you can. Whether you enjoy solo scraps, duo attacks or full-on squad raids, make sure you always have fun the moment your boots hit the ground. That's what Fortnite's No.1 target has always been – to entertain the millions of fans who come back game after game, season after season and year after year. Until next time, keep on battling!

100% UNOFFICIAL